DEDICATED TO ALL REASEARCHERS IN GREEN METHOD

# COSMETIC AND MEDICAL APPLICATIONS OF CHITOSAN COMPOUNDS

A SIMPLE GUIDE TO ALL RESEARCHERS

DR. ADWIN JOSE P

Copyright © Dr. Adwin Jose P
All Rights Reserved.

This book has been published with all efforts taken to make the material error-free after the consent of the author. However, the author and the publisher do not assume and hereby disclaim any liability to any party for any loss, damage, or disruption caused by errors or omissions, whether such errors or omissions result from negligence, accident, or any other cause.

While every effort has been made to avoid any mistake or omission, this publication is being sold on the condition and understanding that neither the author nor the publishers or printers would be liable in any manner to any person by reason of any mistake or omission in this publication or for any action taken or omitted to be taken or advice rendered or accepted on the basis of this work. For any defect in printing or binding the publishers will be liable only to replace the defective copy by another copy of this work then available.

# Contents

# Foreword

Chitosan is a muco-adhesive, non-toxicand biodegradable natural biopolymerthat is prepared from chitin by deacetylation and commercially prepared from shells of shrimp and marine crustaceans. It is a cationic polysaccharide in nature and its chemically modified derivatives are used in a wide range of biological applications such as, antibacterial, antifungal, anticancer, antioxidant, antiviral, drug delivery through the skin, periodontitis, and dental-pulp regeneration. Chitosan has moisture-retention properties, enabling it to act as a skin protectant. The cationic nature of chitosan prevents bacterial growth by disturbing the binding potential of the bacterial membrane. For hair-care purposes, chitosan is an effective film-former and has found use in numerous types of cosmetic formulations. Chitosan compounds are biologically degraded with zero apparent toxicity. Chitosan compounds also act as high-density organic ligands and may be used to stabilize nanoparticles of gold, platinum, palladium silver, copper, and other metals. Carboxymethyl chitosan and its derivatives are widely used in cosmetics applications and have been found to increase the integrity and stability of nanoparticles. Chitosan-capped metal nanoparticles show increased biological activities in various fields. Chitosan-modified compounds have also been employed in various therapeutic processes, e. g. to protect wounds from bacterial infection and to reduce bleeding. In agriculture, chitosan is used to protect against fungal and bacterial infection and helps to prevent spoilage of plants. This article explains the synthesis and biological therapeutic activities of various chitosan compounds.

# Preface

Chitin is an aminopolysaccharide that is widely abundant in the biosphere. Chitin is obtained at an industrial scale from different sources of biomass and food waste (e.g., crustacean and insect exoskeletons, fungi cell walls, and squid pen). Chitosan derived from chitin is water-soluble in acidic conditions and has been used in numerous applications, especially in the biomedical, pharmaceutical, agricultural, and food industries. One of the major remaining issues that has precluded the wider use of chitosan is the difficulty in obtaining a complete and accurate characterization of samples, including the quantities and distribution of the acetyl groups along the chains, the molecular weight distribution, and the choice of a suitable solvent for dissolution. This knowledge allows for assigning a suitable chitosan to fit a given function. Another important issue is the preparation of well-defined derivatives by chemical methods, allowing for a random distribution of the substituents (or grafted chains) along the chains to afford polymers with reproducible properties for specific applications. Many products developed from chitin/chitosan research are innovative biomaterials that are comprised of well-defined chitin and chitosan samples, including films, fibers, nanoparticles, composite materials (involving fibers, solid particles, etc.), hydrogels, polymeric complexes, nanoporous scaffolds, and membranes. The wide range of applications encompass scaffold biomaterials (e.g., in tissue engineering or regenerative medicine), non-viral gene delivery systems, nano- and microparticles for biological transmucosal delivery, fruit and vegetable coatings, biosensors, matrices for water purification, and novel antimicrobials.

# Acknowledgements

First I would like to convey my sincere and deep gratitude to my research supervisor, Dr. J. Dhaveethu Raja M.Sc., M.Phil., Ph.D. Assistant professor, Department of chemistry, The American College, Madurai, for giving me the occasion to give motivation, to write this book and providing precious guidance up to the end.
I express my sincere thanks to the management the Principal of E.G.S. PiLLAY Engineering College, Nagapattinam, for giving me an opportunity to to write this book in this reputed institution.

I am extending my thanks to all Staff members, Department of Science and Humanities (Chemistry, Physics, Mathematics and English) E.G.S. PiLLAY Engineering College, Nagapattinam for their valuable help and suggestions throughout the process.

# Prologue

Chitosan is a biopolymer obtained from chitin, one of the most abundant and renewable materials on Earth. Chitin is a primary component of cell walls in fungi, the exoskeletons of arthropods such as crustaceans, e.g., crabs, lobsters and shrimps, and insects, the radulae of molluscs, cephalopod beaks, and the scales of fsh and lissamphibians. The discovery of chitin in 1811 is attributed to Henri Braconnot while the history of chitosan dates back to 1859 with the work of Charles Rouget. The name of chitosan was, however, introduced in 1894 by Felix Hoppe-Seyler. Chitosan has attracted major scientifc and industrial interests from the late 1970s due to its particular macromolecular structure, biocompatibility, biodegradability and other intrinsic functional properties. Chitosan and derivatives have practical applications in the food industry, agriculture, pharmacy, medicine, cosmetology, textile and paper industries, and in chemistry. In recent years, chitosan has also received much attention in dentistry, ophthalmology, biomedicine and bioimaging, hygiene and personal care, veterinary medicine, packaging industry, agrochemistry, aquaculture, functional textiles and cosmetotextiles, catalysis, chromatography, beverage industry, photography, wastewater treatment and sludge dewatering, and biotechnology. Nutraceuticals and cosmeceuticals are actually growing markets, and therapeutic and biomedical products should be the next markets in the development of chitosan. Chitosan is also the object of numerous fundamental studies. In this book, we highlight a selection of works on chitosan applications published over the past two decades.

CHAPTER ONE

# INTRODUCTION

The development of green technology, side effects and environmental issues associated with products from chemical sources make more and more researchers inclined towards synthesizing medicinal products or cosmetic products from biological sources like plants or animals. Recently, cosmetics from marine resources have emerged as a very effective, low cost, and easily synthesized alternative. Alginate, fucoidans, phlorotannin, and flucoxanthin are obtained from brown algae seaweeds, and carrageenan and mycosporine like amino acids (MAAs) from red algae seaweeds, and ulvans from green algae seaweed. Other marine compounds include glycogen from mussels, aluminum silicate from sea mud, squalene from shark, chitin and chitosan from crustacean shells.

Copolymerization of N-acetyl glucosamine and glucosamine yields chitin. When chitin undergoes deacetylation, the resulting N-deacetylated derivative is called chitosan. Natural chitin is available from some fungi and crustaceans. Chitosan is highly soluble in an aqueous medium. It has two hydroxy functional groups and one amino functional group which readily reacts with other chemical constituents and yields a new derivative. Chitosan derivatives are also bio-friendly materials characterized by their biodegradability, bioadhesiveness, non-toxicity, renewability, and biocompatibility. Cosmetic chitosan is also being used as a therapeutic agent in dental care, skincare, and in other personal care materials.

Cosmetics are generally defined as substances which are prepared to clean and protect external body parts, correct and enhance body odors, modify body appearance, and keep the body in good condition. Cosmetic materials are commonly used in the hair system, lips, nails, epidermis, external genital organs, mucous membrane of the oral cavity, and teeth [1]. Cosmetics are commonly used to decorate the body and are usually applied from the outside. Theyare not beingused to cure and treat diseases.

Cosmetic products are usually tightly regulatedby government authorities.

The term Cosmeceuticals was first introduced in 1980s [2], which have dual properties that are used as cosmetics and as medicines [3].

**Synthesis of chitosan compounds**

Generally, chitosans are naturally prepared from shells of crustaceans species such as crab, lobster, shrimps, etc. Seafood industrial waste is also recycled into environmentally friendly biomaterials and converted to chitosan compounds. Because crustacean shells contain many inorganic salts, lipids, and proteins, the preparation of chitosan is generally carried out in four steps: demineralization, deproteinization, decolorization, and deacetylation [4].

In the first step, shells are collected, rinsed with fresh water, and grained to small size using mechanical motors or by probe sonication. Inorganic carbonate salts are removed by adding hydrochloric acid with constant stirring at ambient temperature. Hydrochloric acid-treated Crustacean shells are then added to a diluted sodium hydroxide solution to remove unwanted proteins and lipids. To remove the color of the chitosan compounds decolorization agents were also added. For 10 kg of 70 % deacetylated chitosan from crustacean shells, 63 kg of hydrochloric acid and 18 kg of sodium hydroxide are needed, as well as the required amounts of water and nitrogen[5].

**Structure of of chitosan**

Chitosan is the deacetylated product of chitin. It has a heterogeneous chemical structure with an amino group as well as hydroxy groups. The two main constituent monomers of chitosan compounds are β-(1→4)-linked D-glucosamine and N-acetyl-D-glucosamine [6]. It has two hydroxy groups and one primary amine for each monomer. Its molecular formula is $C_6H_{11}O_4N$. The structure of chitosan is shown in **Fig.1.**

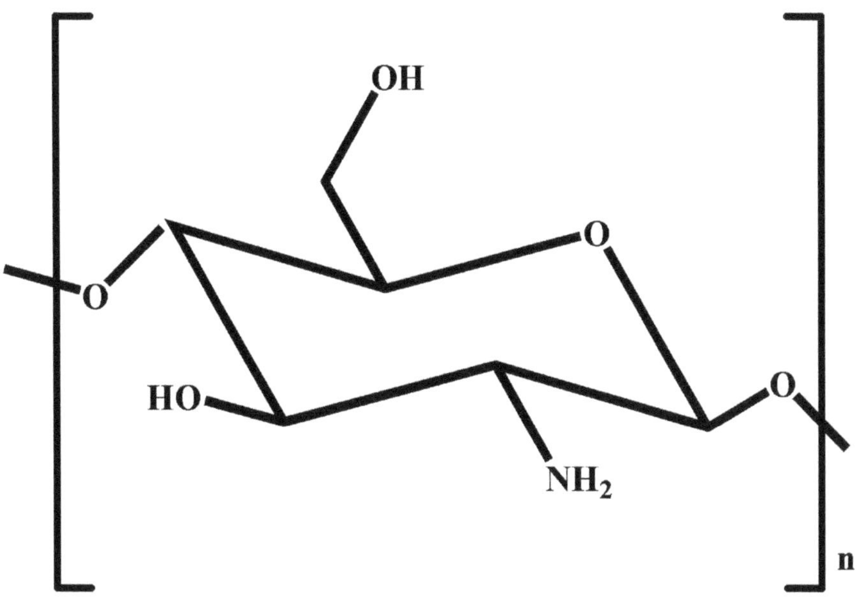


Fig.1. Chemical Structure of Chitosan

CHAPTER TWO

# TYPES OF CHITOSAN COMPOUNDS

**Types of chitosan compounds**

**Acyl chitosans**

Acyl chitosans are synthesized from chitosan by acylation reactions. Acylation with linear or cross-linked long-chain chlorides of aliphatic carboxylic acids togetherwith hexanoyl chlorides, dodecanoyl chlorides, and tetradecanoyl chloridesyieldsderivatives of chitosan with a high degreeof acylation. N-acylation of chitosan with fatty acid chloridesresults in hydrophobic compounds that are highly soluble in chloroform. The structure of acyl chitosan is shown in **Fig.2**. Chitosan with ahighdegreeof deacetylation ismoresusceptible toacylationdue toadecreasein hydrogen bonding. N-acyl chitosan tends to be more stable inthe bodyand more resistant to digestive enzymes such as lysozyme and chitinase, resulting in a greater biocompatibility, compared to normal chitosan [7].

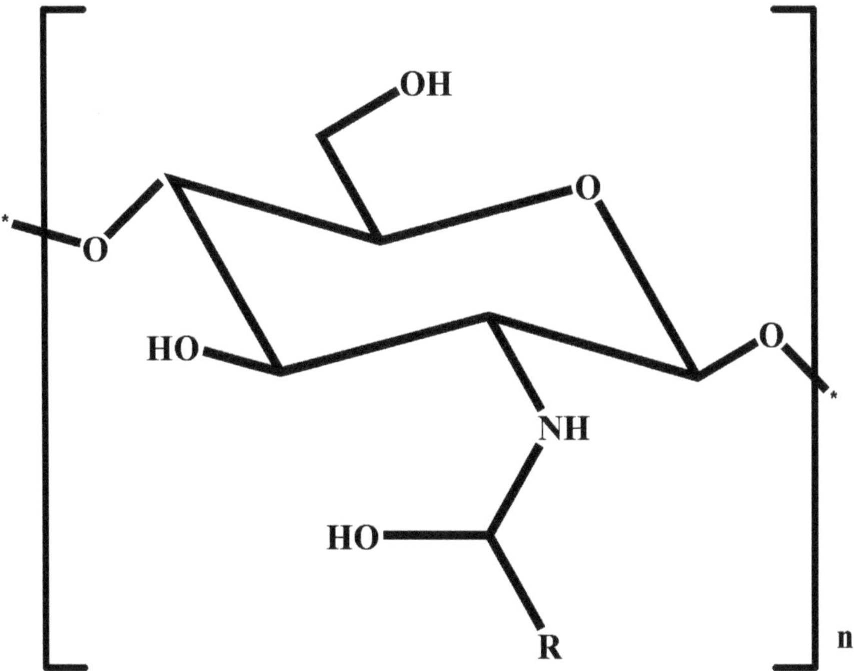


Fig.2.Molecular structure of acyl chitosan monomer.

**Graft copolymer chitosan**

Chitosan and synthetic tailored hybrid polymers under copolymerization yield graft chitosan copolymers. The formation and characteristics of graft copolymers willbe determined by the molecular structure of the reactant, length of the monomer, and the number of functional group side chains attached. Grafting of chitosan allows the formation of many functional derivatives of primary amino chitosan,primary hydroxy chitosan,and secondary hydroxy chitosan. These functional groups interfere with the covalent binding of a molecule to the primary chitosan structure. The swelling character of chitosan has been enhanced by graft polymerization with vinylic monomers such as acrylic acid, acrylamide, and acrylonitrile in an optimum pH range. Superabsorbents have been prepared by grafting these resins with chitosan and have possible applications in infant diapers, feminine hygienc products, agriculture, and other specialized areas [8].

**Carboxymethyl chitosans**

Carboxymethyl chitosan is another derivative of chitosan which is synthesized under defined reaction circumstances and it is shown in **Fig.3**. It can be prepared by alkylation along with reduction of amino chitosan with an aldehyde or else glyoxylic acid and subsequently treated with the strong reducing agent $NaBH_4$ to yield carboxymethyl chitosan. It can also be prepared by direct alkylation using monohalocarboxylic acids such as monochloroacetic acid in an alkaline medium. Carboxymethyl chitosans have improved biological, physical, and chemical characteristics compared to other chitosan compounds when used for a wide range of medicinal applications [9].

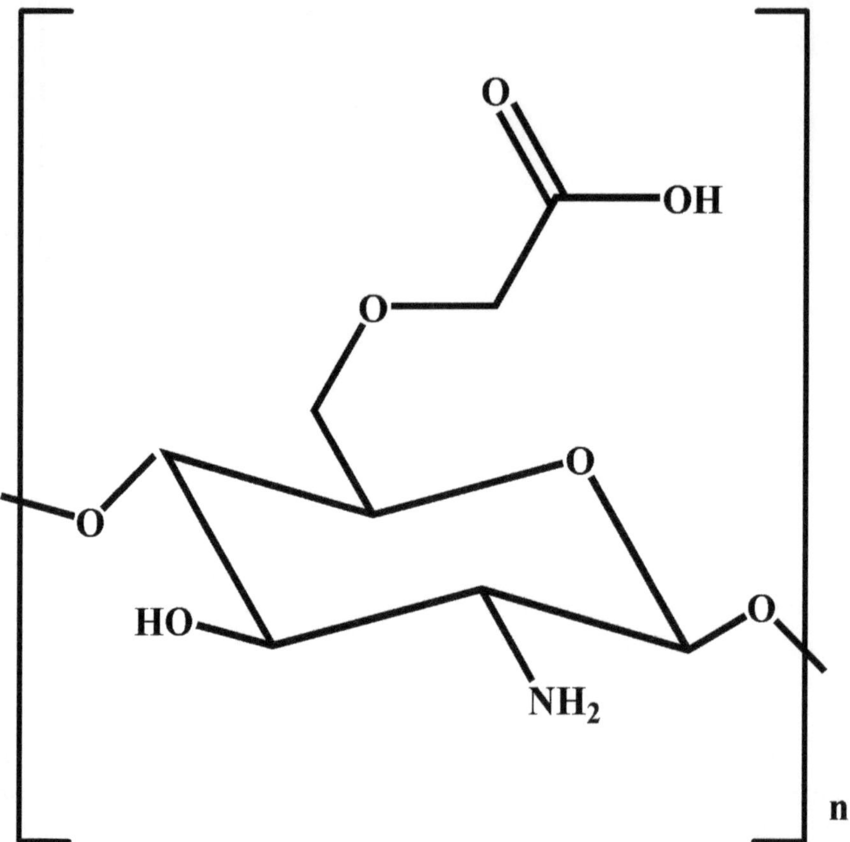


Fig.3. Molecular structure of carboxymethyl chitosan monomer

**N-methylene Phosphonic Chitosans**

This type of chitosan is anionic and amphoteric,and it is shown in **Fig.4**. Itcan be prepared under differentconditions and showsa strong complexation ability with cations of most d-d transition metals. The complexation ability can be exploited for the corrosion protection of metal surfaces. These derivatives can also be customized and alkylated to make them amphiphilic. Thistype of chitosan derivatives is of probablerelevance in cosmetics [10].

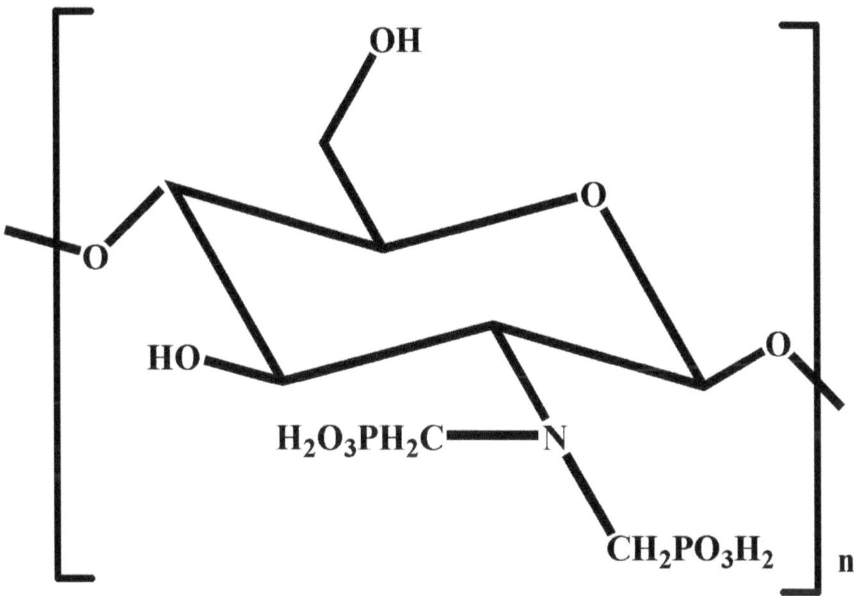


Fig.4. Molecular structure of methylene phosphonic chitosan monomer.

**Carbohydrate Derivatives of Chitosans**

Carbohydrates can be attachedto the chitosan molecule at the second carbon site by reduction followedby alkylation. Using this method, disaccharides can be attached to chitosan in the presence of strong reducing compounds. The resulting derivative is hydrophilic and highly soluble in water. Carbohydrates can also be introducedatthe sixth carbon position of the chitosan molecule without ring opening. A revicw of the literature shows that these chitosansareforemostused in controlled drug delivery[11].

**Alkylated Chitosans**

Alkylated chitosans are exceptionally amphiphilic polymers. They display good surface activity and strongly enhance the viscosity of aqueous solutions, because of their water-repulsive inter-chain relations. Alkylated chitosans are compatible with neutral and cationic surfactants. cationic surfactant adsorbed on the alkyl chain grafted onto chitosan promotes its solubilization[12].

**Hydrophobic Chitosans**

Hydrophobic Chitosan ploymers are highly insoluble in water . Hydrophobic functional derivatives of chitosan can be prepared effortlessly from long-chain acyl chlorides and anhydrides. These chitosans are alsoanticipated to mimic the activities of endotoxins [13].

**Methoxyphenyl Chitosans**

Aldehydes of methoxyphenyl such as vanillin, o-vanillin, syringaldehyde, and veratraldehyde interactwith chitosan spontaneously as well in the presence of reducing agents, yieldingmethoxyphenyl chitosans. Compared to unmodified chitosan, theyshowreducedsolubility and changes inchemical as well as physical characteristics. Methoxyphenyl chitosans obtained from veratraldehyde are highly insoluble, easily biodegradable, stronglymechanically resistant, and environmentally friendly [14].

**Polyurethane-type Chitosans**

Various chitins may be reacted with asurplusof 1,6-diisocyanatohexane to yield polyurethane chitosans. When these polyurethane chitosans are exposed to water vapor, their flexibility and opaquenesswere found to increase. Polyurethane chitosans are insoluble in aqueous medium and in many organic solvents. They are crystalline and show a high degree of substitution. They show no thermoplasticity. When chitosan is treated correspondinglyunder heterogeneous conditions in anhydrous pyridine, ityields reaction products with a lower degree of substitution [15].

**Hydroxyalkyl Chitosans**

When chitosan is reacted with epoxides, it yieldseither N-hydroxyalkyl chitosans, O-hydroxyalkyl chitosans or a mixture of the two. The specific product formed is influenced by the pH of the reaction mixture, the solvent used to carry out the reaction, and the reaction temperature. The reaction may take place mainly at the amino or alcohol functional group of epoxides [16].

**Nanosized Chitosan compounds**

Nanosized chitosan derivatives may be prepared by various methods. Some chitosan nanocomposites are prepared from chitosan with any other substance such as glutaraldehyde, tripolyphosphate, alginate, Arabic gum, carboxymethyl cellulose, carrageenan, chondroitin sulfate, cyclodextrins, dextran sulfate, polyacrylic acid, poly-γ-glutamic acid, insulin, DNA, acrylic acid, methacrylic acid, polyethylene glycol and polyether. Nanosized chitosan derivatives are prepared by physical or chemical methods. Methods include emulsification and cross-linking, emulsion droplet coalescence, emulsion solvent diffusion, reverse micellization, ionic gelation, polyelectrolyte complexation, modified ionic gelation with radical polymerization and desolvation [17]

CHAPTER THREE

# PROPERTIES OF CHITOSAN COMPOUNDS

**Properties of chitosans**

The physical and chemical characteristics of chitosan depend on its molecular weight, degree of crystallinity, degree of deacetylation, availability of free amino groups, the extent of ionization, etc. Different parameters such as reagent type and concentration, reaction time, pH of the reaction mixture, and temperature maintained throughout the reaction will influence the final product [18].

Chitosans are alkaline polysaccharides, in contrast to other biopolymers such as dextran, alginic acid, agar-agar, carrageenan, cellulose, pectin, starch,which are acidic or neutral. Chitosans are easily biodegradable, and most chitosan compounds are odorless. When compared to other natural polymers, chitosans showthe least toxicity. When chitosan derivatives are taken up by humans, theyare decomposed slowly into amino sugars and are completely digested.

**Molecular Weight**

The molecular weight of chitosan is defined by the number of sugar molecules present in the unit volume of polymer chitosan polymer molecules. The physical properties such as solubility, viscosity, elasticity, adsorption, and absorption on solids, tear strength, the biological function will be influenced or changed by the molecular weight of the chitosan. The particle size, surface morphology, crystal size, and grain size of the chitosan plays an important role in the reactivity towards other biological components. The crystallinity of the chitosan derivatives increases with a decrease in molecular weight [19].

### Degree of deacetylation

The degree of deacetylation plays an important role in the solubility, crystallinity and application chitosan based membranes in the filed of reverse osmosis, gas separation, dialysis and pervaporation. The acetyl functionality of chitosans is commonly measured by the degree of deacetylation. Repeating the alkaline treatment of chitosan compounds increases the degree of deacetylation and content of amine groups which are accountable for the adaptability of chitosan. A high degree of deacetylation increases chain length and charge density. Chain flexibility can also be adjusted by changing the degree of deacetylation. High charge density and chain flexibility promote the formation of intramolecular hydrogen bonds. Commonly available chitosans show a degree of deacetylation between 40 to 98 % [20].

### Viscosity

The viscosity of the chitosan compounds always decreases with an increase in temperature and increases with an increase in concentration and degree of deacetylation. Viscosities of chitosans are usually very high because of their high molecular weight and linear structure, enabling them to be used as viscosity increasing agents [21]

### Solubility

The solubility of chitosan is greatly impacted by the pH of the solvent. Chitosans are generally insoluble at pH higher than 7 because of intermolecular hydrogen bonding. Chitosans with a high degree of hydrogen bonding decompose before they reach the melting point. Functional groups present in different chitosans greatly influence the solubility at different pH values. Prolonged stirring increases the solubility of chitosan in some organic and inorganic acids such as lactic acid, phosphoric acid, propionic acid, acetic acid, succinic acid, citric acid tartaric acid, and formic acid. Chitosans also act as chelating agents in neutral solvents, interacting with cationic transition metal ions

CHAPTER FOUR

# COSMETIC APPLICATIONS OF CHITOSAN

**Chitosan in skincare products**

Chitosan is used in lotions, creams, and other cosmetic products. Its cationic character means that it can easily interact with the negatively charged skin surface. Natural chitosan becomes more viscous during acid neutralization. It has a strong moisturizing character, so it is commonly used as a hydrating agent as well as a film-forming substance[23]. Due to its high molecular weight and cationic charge, chitosan remains attached to the skin for a long time. Trans-epidermic water loss decreases when applying high molecular weight chitosan to the skin, resulting in a constant skin humidity and providing softness and flexibility to the skin. Pleasant feeling, smoothness, and flexibility of the skin are enhanced by the film-forming nature of the chitosan, which also protects the skin from harsh environmental conditions. Chitosan has emulsification properties and is used as sun protecting agent. Chitosan has pseudoplastic properties and increases the apparent viscosity of skincare cream or lotions. Skin lotions containing water-soluble chitosan show skin hydration effects that are twice as strong compared to traditional glycerol monostearate [24]. Succinyl chitosan exhibits a stronger moisture-retention character than traditional hyaluronic acid which is also used in pharmaceutical and cosmetics products.

**Chitosan Skin Mask**

Water-soluble chitosans show evidence of good water-holding capacity when mixed withtwo percent methylcellulose which is used in the production of moist masks. For this type of mask, higher molecular weight hydrophilic chitosans can provide an improvedwater-absorbing and retentioncapability [25].

**Chitosans as deodorants**

High molecular weight hydrophilic chitosan shows potentanti-inflammatory characteristics and is used to cure skin irritation. This type of chitosan is used along with alcohol in aftershave lotions. In deodorants, higher molecular weight chitosan compounds are used to attract humidity and reduce water transpiration. Chitosans also have notable antibacterial properties, which gives an additional benefit to chitosan-based deodorant. Nanochitosan and its derivatives were also used in deodorizing products to provide a long-lasting deodorizing result [26].

**Chitosans for skin wound healing**

Chitosan speeds up the wound recuperation process by stimulating inflammatory cells, macrophages, and fibroblasts. The inflammatory period is shortened, and the proliferative phase starts faster within the wound recovery procedure. With the help of chitosans, the formation of fibroblasts is increased and infection was prevented in the newly formed cells. The scar tissue also increased. Chitosan also has the capability to influence granulation tissue formation and angiogenesis, assuring the accurate deposition of collagen fibers and thereby improving the restoration of dermal tissue [27].

In the context of chitosan's wound-healing abilities, it is important to consider its hemostatic and analgesic properties. Chitosan's hemostatic activity is independent of the normal clotting pathways. Furthermore, chitosan can interact with neutrophils and macrophages, influencing the fibroplasia system and re-epithelialization. Chitosan improves fibroblast proliferation, and the proliferative impact appears to be associated with degree of deacetylation. The samples with a high degree of deacetylation amplified the mitogenic activity in fibroblasts, even as chitin had an antiproliferative effect. Probably, the reaction pathway through which chitosan induces fibroblast proliferation proceeds via the formation of polyelectrolyte complexes such as heparin, cytokines, or different proteins at a wounded area [28].

**Chitosan as skin UV protectant**

Chitosan shows not only good adhesive properties, water resistance, and cytocompatibility, but additionally absorbs UV radiation with an absorption maximum at 400 nm. The two UV components in sunlight, UV-A (320 nm to 400 nm) and UV-B (290 nm to 320 nm) cause numerous undesired reactions in skin, including sunburn, pores and skin degeneration, photosensitivity, phototoxicity, photoaging, immuno suppression, and skin cancer. To protect the skin and its pores from exposure to solar radiation, chitosan-containing sunscreens are used [29].

Ito et al. used urocanic acid, the foremost UV-absorbing chromophore in the skin, to prepare urocanic acid-chitin nanofibrils by urocanic acid hydrolysis. They examined the protecting impact of the nanofibrils against UV-B radiation, demonstrating in vivo their protective impact and potential to inhibit erythema prompted by UV-B irradiation and solarization mobile generation[30].

Recently, sunscreen emulsions primarily based on chitosan nanoparticles with a size range between 150–500 nm have been prepared with annatto, ultrafiltered annatto, saffron, and ultrafiltered saffron. All formulations have been synthesized by ionotropic gelation and exhibited appropriate renovation and low toxicity, with solar protection component values ranging from 2.15 to 4.85[31].

**Chitosan as skin cleaning agent**

Chitosans are commonly used for the removal of foreign substances in the skin due to their cationic properties. As positively charged particles, chitosan and its derivatives may be utilized to transport skin cleaning solutions, readily interacting with the anionic skin surface[32].

**Chitosans as skin anti-aging compounds**

Skin aging is a complex processthat is induced by endogenous and exogenous factors like UVradiation, pollution, chemicals,genetic, hormonal and other factors. The wound healing capability of chitosans along with their skin regenerating effectgives them anti-aging properties with regard toskin. Many studies proposed that chitosan increases the lifetime of skin cells and slows downskin aging, adding to the health and beautyof the skin [33].

**Chitosan in dental care products**

Chitosan has been recognized as a potential biomaterial for dental application, thanks to its good bioactivity, significant antimicrobial activity, biocompatibility,and its ability to react or interact with different materials. Chitosan-based materials have been explored for a wide variety of dental applications as detailed in sections 6.2.1 to 6.2.4.

**Additive for Dentifrices**

Tooth pastes are crucial for the everyday oral hygiene. Their function is to prevent dental erosion and demineralization, and to conserve the tooth's shape by counteracting the exposure to acidic foods. The stability of toothpaste formulations has been examined using reactive elements. Ganss and co-workers reported that commercially available dentifrice contains chitosan-based derivatives along with other chemical constituents[34].

**Enamel repair**

The thin outer smooth and hard surface of the teeth is called enamel. Enamel is constantly degraded by chewing, biting, crunching, and grinding. It is a non-vascular and the hardest tissue inthe human body. The enamel coating makesrepair or regeneration of teeth difficult. Some chitosan-based compounds influence tooth enamel regeneration. Ruan and co-workers reported that some chitosan derivative hydrogels are medium for amelogen in delivery to within the crystal structure of teeth. Chitosan has an additional shielding effect against secondary caries due to its antibacterial properties, while maintaining tooth crystal orientation.[35].

**Adhesion and dentine bonding**

The dentine recovery interface and sturdiness of bonding are key issues for dental care scientists. Currently available dentine alternative substances are sensitive to acid etching and removal of the smear layer. Chitosans are commonly used as bonding agents in teeth regeneration. Marina and co-workers reported in 2014 that a methacrylate derivative of chitosan increases the durability of dentine bonding systems. The modified chitosan was used as a constituent of the etching andrinsing adhesive material, efficiently increasing the durability of dental restorations[36].

**Chitosan for dental coating**

The clinical usefulness of dental implants depends on their similarity to the structure and function of living bone and their ability to be firmly embedded in the alveolar bone. Bioactive coatings of dental implants showed increased clinical durability in medically compromised patients and improved their bone health. Some researchers have suggested that chitosan coating of artificial dental implants will be beneficial.

Chitosan coating might also affect the surface and bone interface of teeth via biological changes, mechanical disturbances, and morphological factors. Chitosan coatings change the expansion modulus, there by decreasing the difference between the embedded material and alveolar bone. Furthermore, chitosan coatings can probably be used to impart medicinal properties such as the continued release of antibiotics around the embed area [37].

**Chitosan in hair care products**

Chitosan has a positive charge, enabling it to interact with negatively charged hair. Hair care products containing chitosan have better film-forming properties, compatibility, stiffness, and curl retention than synthetic polymers.[38]. Glyceryl chitosan and its derivatives are used as conditioning agents in hair care products. They have good organoleptic properties and show good tolerance to the anionic surfactants commonly used in shampoos. They are also used in other hair care products such as conditioners, styling agents, and hair oxidizers[39].

The water-soluble chitosan salt that is obtained by neutralizing the free amino acid groups of chitosan with acid hasbeen used as a film-formingagent andstyling agent in hair styling lotions. Its effective concentration is between 0.5% and 1.5%.The additionof conventionalstyling agents allows the product to achievestylingeffectsonfine, soft, and loose hair without making the hair appear unnatural or dull. The productdoes not cause hair stickiness even under high humidity.Importantly, water-soluble chitosan salt can be used by people with a sensitive scalp. Recently, hair styling compositions in the form of creams or gels with up to 3% chitosan and ascorbic acid derived from chitosan ascorbate ion complex without the use of corrosive chemicals have attracted the attention of researchers. [40]

**Chitosan innail care products**

Nail polish is a varnish that can be applied to human nails or toenails to decorate and protect the nail plate. Different polishes have been developed to enhance the decorative effect and to inhibit cracking or peeling. Nail polish consists of a mixture of organic polymers and other ingredients that give it color and texture[41].

In nail care products, dibutylphthalate and camphor are common plasticizers, used to convert the brittle nail into non-brittle films. When mixed with plasticizers, chitosan will enhance the anti-brittleness of the nail in nail lacquers.The action of adhesive polymers ensuring that the nitrocellulose adheres to thebottom of the nail is also increased by chitosan derivatives [42].

Hydroxypropyl chitosan is used forthe distribution of active substances into the nails, based on additives such aswater-solublesynthetic amino-polysaccharide chitosan derivatives. It is characterized by highhydrophilicity, extreme plasticity and a high affinity for keratin. Its wound-restoration activity and compatibility with human tissue make it suitable as a film-forming agent[43].

Hydroxypropyl chitosanaddedas a hydroalcoholicsolutiontobovine hoof slicesformsa thin film after evaporation of the solvent.Thepositivelycharged hydroxypropyl chitosan adheres to the negatively charged keratin of the nail and penetrates the nailstructure,leveling ridges, holes, andotherirregularities. Being water-soluble, the hydroxypropyl chitosan filmiseasilyeliminatedbywashing with water and doesno longerrequire solvents or abrasives[44].

Ciclopirox 8% hydroxypropyl chitosan is a water-soluble original nail polish containing 8% Cyclopirox and hydroxypropyl chitosan. It is a highly transparent solution that can be topically applied to the nails of the hands, feet, and surrounding skin. Ciclopirox 8% hydroxypropyl chitosan dries quickly in a few seconds. After drying, it is odorless and invisible. It can be easily removed by rinsing with water without solvent or nail polish. [45].

CHAPTER FIVE

# CHITOSAN IN ORAL CARE

Chitosan has been proven to reduce the stability of Streptococcus mutans and other microorganisms of the oral cavity. When incorporated into mouthwashes, it can inhibit the formation and adhesion of biofilms. As a hybrid chitosan hydrogel with encapsulated silver nanoparticles, it is an alternative to oral antibacterial operations. Chitosan hydrogels have been proven to have bactericidal propertiesand can release silver nanoparticles for as long as two weeks. They significantly reduce the plaque index and bacteria count. Another study confirmed that chitosan toothpaste can prevent dental erosion. [46].

Schuster et al. showed that effectiveness of tin or tin toothpaste and chitosan fluoride in the case of dental erosion or allergic reactions. In another study, Uysal and colleagues achieved the same results, showing that toothpaste containing chitosan can reduce tooth demineralization in patients with poor oral hygiene[47].

When the effect of chitosan mouthwash was compared with two other types of mouthwash on the market, it could be shown that the chitosan-containing mouthwash can simultaneously inhibit the adhesion of microorganisms, the formation of biofilms, and mature biofilms, recommending it as a natural and effective alternative to traditional mouthwash [48].

Lip care products are often used to prevent moisture loss, which can lead to chapped lips. The main additives in lipstick formulations are wax and oil, with additional lip care ingredients including UV filters and lipophilic active ingredients. The addition of chitosan is believed to induce different types of pores and skin patterns and play a role in wound healing. One study on the effect of chitosan on fibroblasts showed an improvement in mobile adhesion, confirming the application prospects of chitosan as an active ingredient in lip care. The addition of chitosan can soften the lips and help maintain their color for an extended time [49].

**Chitosan in caries treatment**

Dental caries is one of the most common oral health problems worldwide. It is a pathological condition caused by organic acids produced by plaque biofilm. It is a dynamic process related to the imbalance between demineralization and remineralization and must be treated with a remineralization agent [50].

H. Jiankang et al recently reported an anti-caries device that can prevent dental caries, treat early tooth decay and white lesions as well as promote remineralization. The mineral solution of carboxymethyl chitosan/ amorphous calcium phosphate (CMC/ACP) nanocomposite has been previously characterized and its antibacterial activity was evaluated on enamel-coated saliva. The results showed that the adhesion of Streptococcus mutants and Streptococcus Gordonii was inhibited by 90% and 86%, and biofilm formation was reduced by about 45% and 44% [51].

In addition, CMC/ACP reduced the binding of Fusobacterium nucleatum (biofilm-enhancing promoter) to streptococcal biofilm by 75%, as was evident from the zeta capacity of bacterial suspension and cytochrome-bound bacteria. Achmad et al. synthesized a toothpaste based on white shrimp (Litopenaeus vannamei) chitosan (5%), which reduced the number of Streptococcus mutant colonies in early childhood tooth decay. [52].

**Chitosans inerosive tooth care**

Erosion of dental material is also caused by chemical and mechanical processes that are not related to bacteria. In a study published in 2018, researchers examined the preventive effect of toothpaste on permanent teeth and temporary tooth enamel for the first time. They found that the initial microhardness of the surface of temporary enamel is lower than that of permanent teeth [53]. When using fluoride toothpaste (four unique formulas), there was no significant difference between the two tooth types, but when treated with a fluoride-free placebo toothpaste, the temporary teeth showed significantly better results than the permanent enamel.

The presence of chitosan as a thickener in anti-erosion toothpaste provides a greater preventive effect on deciduous teeth, while the NaF anti-erosion toothpaste formula appears to have equal performance with both types of tooth enamel. Beltrami and co-workers studied the in vitro anti-erosion effect of phosphorylated chitosan solution in bovine dentin.

Profilometry, nano-hardness, and scanning electron microscopy (SEM) were used to measure dental pulp loss, dental pulp hardness, and elastic modulus, confirming the preventive effect of chitosan treatment for tooth erosion [54].

**Chitosans in gingivitis care**

An oral disease associated with lichen planus is desquamative gingivitis, in which the gums are infected, swollen, and red. Desquamative gingivitis can be treated with topical corticosteroids, including hydrocortisone sodium succinate, a water-soluble artificial by-product of hydrocortisone [55].

Davoudi and co-workers reported the use of an environmentally friendly chitosan/gelatin/keratin composite method containing hydrocortisone sodium succinate as an oral mucosal adhesion cream to treat the oral pH of desquamative gingivitis [56].

**Chitosan inperiodontitis care**

Periodontal disease, also known as gum disease, is a serious gum infection that can damage soft tissues and, if left untreated, can damage the bones that support the teeth. Periodontal disease can cause loose enamel or tooth loss. This includes damage to the dental system (loss of alveolar bone, fracture of periodontal ligament), which can lead to true tooth loss. Anti-inflammatory diseases can be treated with statin tablets containing atorvastatin [57].

To increase the effectiveness of the drug and improve in situ processing, a bioadhesive transport device based entirely on chitosan was developed for the targeted application of atorvastatin. A suitable viscosity and residence time of the bioadhesive was determined, which is beneficial for cleaning applications of periodontal pocket expansion and sustained drug release. The use of human gingival fibroblasts showed that the release of cytokines was reduced by the action of atorvastatin, and the presence of chitosan increased anti-inflammatory activity [58].

**Chitosan in bone tissue engineering**

Bone is a strong connective tissue with special functions, which constitutes the human skeletal structure, supports the muscular system, protects vital organs, and participates in phosphorus and calcium homeostasis and other physiological functions. When faced with moderate, short length defects, bone tissue shows a self-repair ability due to the osteogenic differentiation of bone marrow mesenchymal stem cells, new bone formation, and angiogenesis in specific parts. [59].

In the bone structure, the physiological inertness and toxic effects of scaffolds made from a framework mainly based on chitosan have been proven by a large number of in vitro and in vivo studies. Tissues with chitosan as the main component will not cause allergic and inflammatory reactions during implantation, injection, or topical application. Once installed, however, the use of chitosan as a scaffold is limited due to its reduced biological activity and mechanical properties. By combining chitosan scaffolds with various synthetic or natural polymers (such as polyvinyl alcohol, polycaprolactone, algae, collagen, silk) these shortcomings can be overcome. [60].

Every in vitro and in vivo experiment has so far confirmed that chitosan-based all-biocomposite scaffolds are non-toxic and have excellent biocompatibility, osteo conductivity, and osteogenic properties, allowing proper cell proliferation and promoting adhesion, which in turn promotesnew boneformation. With regard to chitosan-based scaffolds for the regeneration of jaw and alveolar bone, many preclinical reviews have shown promising effects, including accelerated osseointegration of dental implants and reconstruction of large defects [61].

Natural chitosan is a suitable substrate for osteoblast adhesion and proliferation, as well as matrix formation and mineralization, but the electrical and structural stability of natural chitosan scaffolds is usually insufficient for bone engineering projects. Calcium phosphate in the micro- or nanometer range generally has higher mechanical and biological stability than a pure chitosan backbone. Although progress has been made in improving the compressibility of natural chitosan scaffolds, the addition of two-dimensional elements, including alginate and/or nano-hydroxyapatite, seems to indicate significant changes in scaffold structural stability and osteogenic response. In recent years, the mixture of chitosan and bioactive ceramics has been proven to play an important role in bone engineering, because these compounds have good physical, biological, and mechanical properties for bone regenerationand show a predictable degradation behavior

CHAPTER SIX

# ANTI MICROBIAL AND ANTI OXIDANT ACTIVITIES OF CHITOSAN COMPOUNDS

**Antimicrobial activity of chitosan compounds**

One of the most studied properties of chitosan is its antibacterial effect, which is important for many applications, ranging from biomedical to cosmetics, food, and agriculture. So far, to take advantage of the antibacterial properties of chitosan and its unique ability to produce self-preservative substances, a lot of research has been conducted, leading to the development of a variety of products containing chitosan in the form of pearls. Films, fibers, membranes, and hydrogels can also be used for a variety of purposes. In experiments on the interaction with special forms of chitosan in vivo and in vitro, chitosan has been studied as an antimicrobial compound with activity against a large number of target organisms, such as algae, bacteria, yeast, and fungi [63].

The exact mechanism of the antibacterial effect is not fully understood. It is known, however, that the antibacterial activity of chitosan is stimulated by many factors and that the structure of chitosan is a prerequisite for its antibacterial properties. Membrane permeability, along with DNA binding, leads to inhibition of DNA replication and ultimately cell death. Another possible mechanism is that chitosan acts as a chelating agent and selectively binds to trace metals to induce toxin production and inhibit microbial growth. Surface proteinsalso play an important role for its antibacterial activity [64].

Chitosans form a polycationic structure under acidic conditions because the grafted group of the respective derivative can change the pKa value and thus the protonation state of chitosan at a wider pH range. With the increase of chitosan charge density, the antibacterial properties increase correspondingly, as seen in quaternized chitosan and composite chitosan steel. If the polycationic properties of chitosan are reduced or removed, the corresponding antibacterial potential will be weakened or lost. In addition to protonation, the number of functional amino groups bound to C2 in the chitosan backbone is also critical for electrostatic interactions. A large number of amino-functional groups may improve antibacterial activity [65].

Therefore, topical chitosan with better deacetylation(DD) shows a stronger inhibitory effect than molecules with lower DD. In addition, it was postulated that N-asparagine-coupled chitosan oligosaccharides with two final potential points will strongly interact with the carboxyl groups in the mobile bacterial wall. Further attempts to increase the number of functional amino groups by replacing formamidine with amino groups have resulted in the production of guanidine chitosan, which shows better antibacterial activity than chitosan [66].

**Antioxidant activity of chitosan compounds**

Chitosan and its derivatives show antoxidant activity by scavenging specific types of oxygen free radicals (including alkyl, superoxide, hydroxyl, and 2,2-diphenylpicrylhydrazine). The mechanism is still in doubt, but it must be related to chelation. Un stable Free radical ions reacts with hydroxyl and amino polysaccharide drugs, resulting in the formation of stable substance [67]. The invitro control showed that the high probability of DD and low molecular weight increases the antioxidant activity.A good example is provided to illustrate the decomposition of chitosan as a potential source of antioxidants for cosmetic items. Phosrithong et al.used ion exchange technology to synthesize three different mixtures of N, N, and N-trimethyl chitosan salts with acetylsalicylate, ascorbate, citrate, and gallate. The coordinated ligand of acidic anions and trimethylchitosan cations inhibit free radical chain reactions [68].

Chitosan can also be used to provide liposome delivery systems for anti-aging cosmetic formulations. A study showed that a liposomal chitosan preparation has low cytotoxicity and acts as a powerful anti-oxidant for removing reactive oxygen species from $H_2O_2$ [69].

CHAPTER SEVEN

# CONCLUSION

The natural biopolymer chitosan is a muco-adhesive, non-toxic, and biodegradable compound that is prepared from chitin by deacetylation process and commercially prepared from shells of shrimp and some sea crustaceans. It is in cationic polysaccharide in its natural form, and its chemically modified derivatives are used in a wide range of biological applications such as antibacterials, antifungals, anticancer compounds, antioxidants, antivirals, drug delivery through the skin, periodontitis, and dentalpulp regeneration. Carboxymethyl chitosan and its derivatives are also widely used in cosmetics applications. Chitosan has moisture-retention properties, so it canact as a skin protectant. For hair-care purposes, chitosan is a tremendous filmformer and has found use in numerous types of cosmetic formulations. The cationic nature of chitosan prevents bacterial growth by disturbing the binding potential of the bacterial membrane. Chitosan compounds arereadily degraded by many enzymes, resulting in their high biodegradability and zero biological toxicity.

# References

[1]Ta Quynh, Jessica Ting, Sophie Harwood, Nicola Browning, Alan Simm, Kehinde Ross, Ivan Olier, and Raida Al-Kassas. "Chitosan Nanoparticles for Enhancing Drugs and Cosmetic Components Penetration through the Skin" European Journal of Pharmaceutical Sciences, 160 (2021) 105765.

[2] Bhardwaj Shubhang, Nishi Kant Bhardwaj, and Yuvraj Singh Negi. "Surface Coating of Chitosan of Different Degree of Acetylation on Non Surface Sized Writing and Printing Grade Paper." Carbohydrate Polymers, 269 (2021) 117674.

[3] B. Krishnaveni."Chitosan: A Review on its Varied Novel Therapeutic and Industrial Applications" Journal of Drug Delivery and Therapeutics, 6, 6 (2016).

[4] Sajid Muhammad Aamir, Sohail Anjum Shahzad, Fatima Hussain, W. G. Skene, Zulfiqar Ali Khan, and Muhammad Yar. "Synthetic Modifications of Chitin and Chitosan as Multipurpose Biopolymers: A Review" Synthetic Communications, 48, 15 (2018) 1893–1908.

[5] Trang Si Trung, Le Huyen Tram, Nguyen Van Tan, Nguyen Van Hoa, Nguyen Cong Minh, Phan Thanh Loc, and Willem F. Stevens. "Improved Method for Production of Chitin and Chitosan from Shrimp Shells" Carbohydrate Research 489 (2020) 107913.

[6] Mudasir Ahmad, Kaiser Manzoor, Sandeep Singh, and Saiqa Ikram. "Chitosan Centered Bionanocomposites for Medical Specialty and Curative Applications: A Review" International Journal of Pharmaceutics, 529, 1–2 (2017) 200–217.

[7] S. Hirano and Y. Yagi, "The effects of N-substitution of chitosan and the physical form of the products on the rate of hydrolysis by chitinase from Streptomyces griseus" Carbohydrate Research, 8 (1980) (1) 103–108.

[8]S. P. Chawla, S. R. Kanatt, and A. K. Sharma, "Chitosan" Polysaccharides, 2014 1–24.

[9] Z. Shariatinia, "Carboxymethyl chitosan: Properties and biomedical applications," International Journal of Biological Macromolecules, 120 (2018) 1406–1419.

[10] A. Heras, "N-methylene phosphonic chitosan: a novel soluble derivative" Carbohydrate Polymers, 44, 1 (2001) 1–8.

[11] M. Morimoto, H. Saimoto, H. Usui, Y. Okamoto, S. Minami, and Y. Shigemasa, "Biological Activities of Carbohydrate-Branched Chitosan

Derivatives" Biomacromolecules, 2, 4(2001) 1133–1136.

[12] J. Desbrieres, C. Martinez, and M. Rinaudo, "Hydrophobic Derivatives of Chitosan: Characterization and Rheological Behaviour" International Journal of Biological Macromolecules 19, 1 (1996) 21–28.

[13] P. Urrutia, R. Arrieta, L. Alvarez, C. Cardenas, M. Mesa, and L. Wilson, "Immobilization of Lipases in Hydrophobic Chitosan for Selective Hydrolysis of Fish Oil: The Impact of Support Functionalization on Lipase Activity, Selectivity and Stability" International Journal of Biological Macromolecules, 108 (2018) 674–686.

[14] G.F. Payne, M.V. Chaubal, and T. A. Barbari, "Enzyme-Catalysed Polymer Modification: Reaction of Phenolic Compounds with Chitosan Films" Polymer, 37, 20 (1996): 4643–4648.

[15] Groboillot, A. F., C. P. Champagne, G. D. Darling, D. Poncelet, and R. J. Neufeld, "Membrane Formation by Interfacial Cross-Linking of Chitosan for Microencapsulation ofLactococcus Lactis" Biotechnology and Bioengineering, 42, 10 (1993) 1157–1163.

[16] Shanta Pokhrel, and Paras Nath Yadav, "Functionalization of Chitosan Polymer and Their Applications" Journal of Macromolecular Science: Part A, 56, 5 (2019) 450–475.

[17] Grenha, Ana, "Chitosan Nanoparticles: a Survey of Preparation Methods" Journal of Drug Targeting, 20, 4 (2012) 291–300.

[18] W.J. Hennen, "Chitosan natural fat blocker" Woodland Publishing, Salt Lake City, 1996.

[19] K. C. Gupta, and F. H. Jabrail, "Effect of Molecular Weight and Degree of Deacetylation on Controlled Release of Isoniazid from Chitosan Microspheres." Polymers for Advanced Technologies 19, 5 (2008) 432–441.

[20] C. Chatelet, "Influence of the Degree of Acetylation on Some Biological Properties of Chitosan Films." Biomaterials 22, 3 (2001) 261–268.

[21]KazunoriYamada, Tianhong Chen, Guneet Kumar, Oleg Vesnovsky, L. D. Timmie Topoleski, and G.F.Payne, "Chitosan Based Water-Resistant Adhesive. Analogy to Mussel Glue" Biomacromolecules, 1, 2 (2000) 252–258.

[22]Feng, Yongwei, and Wenshui Xia, "Preparation, Characterization and Antibacterial Activity of Water-Soluble O-Fumaryl-Chitosan" Carbohydrate Polymers, 83, 3 (2011) 1169–1173.

[23] InmaculadaAranaz, Niuris Acosta, Concepcion Civera, Begona Elorza, Javier Mingo, Carolina Castro, Maria Gandia, and Angeles Heras

Caballero,"Cosmetics and Cosmeceutical Applications of Chitin, Chitosan and Their Derivatives" Polymers 10, 2 (2018) 213.

[24] Peipei Feng, Yang Luo, Chunhai Ke, Haofeng Qiu, Wei Wang, Yabin Zhu, Ruixia Hou, Long Xu, and Songze Wu, "Chitosan-Based Functional Materials for Skin Wound Repair: Mechanisms and Applications" Frontiers in Bioengineering and Biotechnology 9 (2021) 111.

[25] C.R. Afonso, R.S. Hirano, A.L. Gaspar, E.G.L. Chagas, R.A. Carvalho, F.V. Silva, G.R. Leonardi, P.S. Lopes, C.F. Silva, and C.M.P. Yoshida. "Biodegradable Antioxidant Chitosan Films Useful as an Anti-Aging Skin Mask, " International Journal of Biological Macromolecules 132 (2019) 1262–1273.

[26] Rouhani Shirvan, Anahita, Mina Shakeri, and Azadeh Bashari, "Recent Advances in Application of Chitosan and Its Derivatives in Functional Finishing of Textiles" The Impact and Prospects of Green Chemistry for Textile Technology (2019) 107–133.

[27] Jiahui He, Yongping Liang, Mengting Shi, and Baolin Guo. "Anti-Oxidant Electroactive and Antibacterial Nanofibrous Wound Dressings Based on Poly(ε-Caprolactone)/quaternized Chitosan-Graft-Polyaniline for Full-Thickness Skin Wound Healing" Chemical Engineering Journal 385 (2020) 123464.

[28] Robin Augustine, Syed Raza Ur Rehman, Rashid Ahmed, Alap Ali Zahid, Majid Sharifi, Mojtaba Falahati, and Anwarul Hasan. "Electrospun Chitosan Membranes Containing Bioactive and Therapeutic Agents for Enhanced Wound Healing" International Journal of Biological Macromolecules 156 (2020) 153–170.

[29] Mona Verma, Neha Gahlot, Saroj S. Jeet Singh, and Neelam M. Rose, "UV Protection and Antibacterial Treatment of Cellulosic Fibre (cotton) Using Chitosan and Onion Skin Dye" Carbohydrate Polymers, 257 (2021) 117612.

[30] I. Ito, T. Yoneda, Y. Omura, T. Osaki, S. Ifuku, H. Saimoto, K. Azuma, T. Imagawa, T. Tsuka, Y. Murahata, N. Ito, Y. Okamoto, and S. Minami, "Protective Effect of Chitin Urocanate Nanofibers against Ultraviolet Radiation," Marine Drugs, 13 (12) 2015 7463–7475.

[31]. S. Ntohogian, V. Gavriliadou, E. Christodoulou, S. Nanaki, S. Lykidou, P. Naidis, L. Mischopoulou, P. Barmpalexis, N. Nikolaidis, and D. Bikiaris, "Chitosan Nanoparticles with Encapsulated Natural and UF-Purified Annatto and Saffron for the Preparation of UV Protective Cosmetic Emulsions," Molecules, 23 (9) 2018, 2107.

[32]Aachmann Matica, Tondervik, Sletta, and Ostafe. "Chitosan as a Wound Dressing Starting Material: Antimicrobial Properties and Mode of Action" International Journal of Molecular Sciences, 20, 23 (2019) 5889.

[33] Kaihang Chen, Binzhao Guo, and Jiwen Luo. "Quaternized Carboxymethyl Chitosan/organic Montmorillonite Nanocomposite as a Novel Cosmetic Ingredient Against Skin Aging" Carbohydrate Polymers 173 (2017) 100–106.

[34] C. Ganss, J. Klimek, and N. Schlueter, "Erosion/Abrasion-Preventing Potential of NaF and F/Sn/Chitosan Toothpastes in Dentine and Impact of the Organic Matrix," Caries Research, 48 (2) 2014 163–169..

[35] Q. Ruan, Y. Zhang, X. Yang, S. Nutt, and J. Moradian-Oldak, "An amelogenin–chitosan matrix promotes assembly of an enamel-like layer with a dense interface," Acta Biomaterialia, 9 (7), 2013 7289–7297.

[36] D. Marina, I. Donati, G. Turco, M. Cadenaro, R. Di Lenarda, L. Breschi, and S. Paoletti, "Use of Methacrylate-Modified Chitosan to Increase the Durability of Dentine Bonding Systems" Biomacromolecules, 15 (12) 2014, 4606–4613.

[37] Ramasubba Reddy Palem, Nabanita Saha, Ganesh D. Shimoga, Zuzana Kronekova, Monika Slavikova, and Petr Saha. "Chitosan–silver Nanocomposites: New Functional Biomaterial for Health-Care Applications" International Journal of Polymeric Materials and Polymeric Biomaterials, 67, 1 (2017) 1–10.

[38] Pierfrancesco Morganti, Gianluca Morganti, and Maria-Beatrice Coltelli. "Smart and Sustainable Hair Products Based on Chitin-Derived Compounds" Cosmetics, 8,1 (2021) 20.

[39] Mihai Chirita, "Mechanical Properties of Collagen Biomimetic Films Formed in the Presence of Calcium, Silica and Chitosan" Journal of Bionic Engineering 5, 2 (2008) 149–158. [40] Alina Sionkowska, Beata Kaczmarek, Marta Michalska, Katarzyna Lewandowska, and Sylwia Grabska. "Preparation and Characterization of Collagen/chitosan/hyaluronic Acid Thin Films for Application in Hair Care Cosmetics" Pure and Applied Chemistry, 89, 12 (2017) 1829–1839.

[41] M. A Ghannoum, L. Long, N. Isham, A. Bulgheroni, M. Setaro, M. Caserini, R. Palmieri, and F. Mailland, "Ability of Hydroxypropyl Chitosan Nail Lacquer To Protect Against Dermatophyte Nail Infection" Antimicrobial Agents and Chemotherapy, 59, 4 (2014) 1844–1848.

[42] Bianca Maria Piraccini, Matilde Iorizzo, André Lencastre, Pietro Nenoff, and Dimitris Rigopoulos, "Ciclopirox Hydroxypropyl Chitosan

(HPCH) Nail Lacquer: A Review of Its Use in Onychomycosis" Dermatology and Therapy, 10, 5 (2020) 917–929.

[43]Renata Palmieri, Franca Cantoresi, Maurizio Caserini, Antonella Bidoli, Francesca Maggio, Raffaella Marino, Claudia Carnevale, and Paola Sorgi, "Randomized Controlled Trial of a Water-Soluble Nail Lacquer Based on Hydroxypropyl-Chitosan (HPCH), in the Management of Nail Psoriasis" Clinical, Cosmetic and Investigational Dermatology, 7 (2014) 185-190

[44] Daniela Monti, L. Saccomani, P. Chetoni, S. Burgalassi, M. F. Saettone, and F. Mailland, "In Vitro Transungual Permeation of Ciclopirox from a Hydroxypropyl Chitosan-Based, Water-Soluble Nail Lacquer." Drug Development and Industrial Pharmacy, 31, 1 (2005) 11–17.

[45] D. Monti, U. Herranz, L. Dal Bo, and A. Subissi, "Nail Penetration and Predicted Mycological Efficacy of an Innovative Hydrosoluble Ciclopirox Nail Lacquer Vs. a Standard Amorolfine Lacquer in Healthy Subjects." Journal of the European Academy of Dermatology and Venereology, 27, 2 (2012) e153–e158.

[46] Shigehiro Hirano, Haruyoshi Seino, Yasutoshi Akiyama, and Isao Nonaka. "Chitosan: A Biocompatible Material for Oral and Intravenous Administrations," Progress in Biomedical Polymers, (1990) 283–290.

[47] T. Uysal, M. D. Akkurt, M. Amasyali, S. Ozcan, A. Yagci, F. Basak, and D. Sagdic, "Does a chitosan-containing dentifrice prevent demineralization around orthodontic brackets?," The Angle Orthodontist, 81 (2) 2011 319–325.

[48]E.M. Costa, S. Silva, A.R. Madureira, A. Cardelle-Cobas, F.K. Tavaria, and M.M. Pintado, "A comprehensive study into the impact of a chitosan mouthwash upon oral microorganism's biofilm formation in vitro" Carbohydrate Polymers, 101 (2014) 1081-1086.

[49] G. Singh Dhillon, S. Kaur, S. Jyoti Sarma, S. Kaur Brar, M. Verma, and R. Yadagiri Surampalli, "Recent Development in Applications of Important Biopolymer Chitosan in Biomedicine, Pharmaceuticals and Personal Care Products," Current Tissue Engineering, 2 (1) 2013, 20–40 .[50] T. M. S. Arnaud, B. de Barros Neto, and F. B. Diniz, "Chitosan effect on dental enamel de-remineralization: An in vitro evaluation," Journal of Dentistry, 3, (2010) 848–852. [51] H. Jiankang, Y. Bao, J. Li, Z. Qiu, Y. Liu, and X. Zhang, "Nanocomplexes of carboxymethyl chitosan/amorphous calcium phosphate reduce oral bacteria adherence and biofilm formation on human enamel surface," Journal of Dentistry, 80 (2019) 15–22.

[52] Y. F. Ramadhany, H. Achmad, P. Khairunnisa, and M. Mardiana, "The Efficacy of Chitosan Toothpaste Based White Shrimp (Litopenaeus Vannamei) to Decrease Streptococcus Mutans Colonies in Children with Early Childhood Caries," Proceedings of the 11th International Dentistry Scientific Meeting (IDSM 2017), 2018.

[53] N. G. Emerenciano, A. C. Botazzo Delbem, J. P. Pessan, G. P. Nunes, F. N. Souza Neto, E. R. de Camargo, and M. Danelon, "In situ effect of fluoride toothpaste supplemented with nano-sized sodium trimetaphosphate on enamel demineralization prevention and biofilm composition," Archives of Oral Biology, 96 (2018) 223–229.[54] A. P. C. A. Beltrame, D. Suchyta, I. Abd Alraheam, A. Mohammed, M. Schoenfisch, R. Walter, I. C. S. Almeida, L. C. Souza, and P. A. Miguez, "Effect of Phosphorylated Chitosan on Dentin Erosion: An in vitro Study," Caries Research, 52 (2018) 378–386.

[55] Wikanta, Thamrin, Erizal Erizal, and Sugiyono Sugiyono. "Chitosan Composite of Crab Shell and Hydroxyapatite of Tuna Fish Bone as Biomaterials for Guided Tissue Regeneration" Squalen Bulletin of Marine and Fisheries Postharvest and Biotechnology 8, 1 (2014).

[56] Zahra Davoudi, Mohammad Rabiee, Behzad Houshmand, Niloofar Eslahi, Kimia Khoshroo, Morteza Rasoulianboroujeni, Mohammadreza Tahriri, and Lobat Tayebi, "Development of Chitosan/gelatin/keratin Composite Containing Hydrocortisone Sodium Succinate as a Buccal Mucoadhesive Patch to Treat Desquamative Gingivitis" Drug Development and Industrial Pharmacy, 44, 1 (2017) 40–55.

[57] Yuqian Hu, Yan Chen, Lijuan Lin, Jinhui Zhang, Rengang Lan, and Buling Wu, "Studies on Antimicrobial Peptide-Loaded Nanomaterial for Root Caries Restorations to Inhibit Periodontitis Related Pathogens in Periodontitis Care" Journal of Microencapsulation,38, 2 (2021) 89–99.

[58] Qiu Xia Ji, Jing Deng, Xiao Ming Xing, Chang Qing Yuan, Xin Bo Yu, Quan Chen Xu, and Jin Yue, "Biocompatibility of a Chitosan-Based Injectable Thermosensitive Hydrogel and Its Effects on Dog Periodontal Tissue Regeneration." Carbohydrate Polymers, 82, 4 (2010) 1153–1160.

[59] Jayachandran Venkatesan, and Se-Kwon Kim, "Chitosan Composites for Bone Tissue Engineering—An Overview" Marine Drugs, 8, 8 (2010) 2252–2266.

[60] F. Chicatun, G. Griffanti, M.D. McKee, and S.N. Nazhat, "Collagen/chitosan Composite Scaffolds for Bone and Cartilage Tissue Engineering" Biomedical Composites, (2017) 163–198.

[61] Robert Adamski, and Dorota Siuta, "Mechanical, Structural, and Biological Properties of Chitosan/Hydroxyapatite/Silica Composites for Bone Tissue Engineering" Molecules, 26, 7 (2021) 1976.

[62] E.I. Akpan, O.P. Gbenebor, S.O. Adeosun, and Odili Cletus, "Chitin and Chitosan Composites for Bone Tissue Regeneration" Handbook of Chitin and Chitosan, (2020) 499–553. [63] AlessandroMartins, Suelen Facchi, Heveline Follmann, Antonio Pereira, Adley Rubira, and Edvani Muni, "Antimicrobial Activity of Chitosan Derivatives Containing N-Quaternized Moieties in Its Backbone: A Review" International Journal of Molecular Sciences. 15, 11 (2014): 20800–20832.

[64] Atay Yilmaz and Husnugul, "Antibacterial Activity of Chitosan-Based Systems." Functional Chitosan (2019) 457–489.

[65] Chin-San Wu, "Characterization and Antibacterial Activity of Chitosan-Based Composites with Polyester" Polymers for Advanced Technologies, 23, 3 (2011) 463–469.

[66] Alireza Joorabloo, Zohreh Mansoori-Moghadam, Armaghan Moghaddam, and Mohammad Taghi Khorasani, "Physical Properties and Antibacterial Activity of Chitosan/Carboxymethyl Cellulose/Starch Biofilms as Natural Bio-Based Polymers" Eco-Friendly and Smart Polymer Systems (2020) 56–59.

[67] CahitDemetgul, and Neslihan Beyazit. "Synthesis, Characterization and Antioxidant Activity of Chitosan-Chromone Derivatives." Carbohydrate Polymers 181 (2018) 812–817.

[68] Narumol Phosrithong, Weerasak Samee, Patcharawee Nunthanavanit, and Jiraporn Ungwitayatorn. "In Vitro Antioxidant Activity Study of Novel Chromone Derivatives" Chemical Biology & Drug Design, 79, 6 (2012) 981–989.

[69] Xueqi Sun, Jingjing Zhang, Yuan Chen, Yingqi Mi, Wenqiang Tan, Qing Li, Fang Dong, and Zhanyong Guo, "Synthesis, Characterization, and the Antioxidant Activity of Carboxymethyl Chitosan Derivatives Containing Thiourea Salts" Polymers, 11, 11 (2019) 1810.

www.ingramcontent.com/pod-product-compliance
Ingram Content Group UK Ltd.
Pitfield, Milton Keynes, MK11 3LW, UK
UKHW041849190726
13854UKWH00002B/787

9 798887 172453